Five Years of Solitary

By

Elliot Torres

Copyright © 2002 by Elliot Torres

All rights reserved. No part of this book shall be reproduced or transmitted in any form or by any means, electronic, mechanical, magnetic, photographic including photocopying, recording or by any information storage and retrieval system, without prior written permission of the publisher. No patent liability is assumed with respect to the use of the information contained herein. Although every precaution has been taken in the preparation of this book, the publisher and author assume no responsibility for errors or omissions. Neither is any liability assumed for damages resulting from the use of the information contained herein.

This is a work of fiction. Names, characters, places, and incidents either are the product of the author's imagination or are used fictitiously. Any resemblance to actual events or locales or persons, living or dead, is entirely coincidental.

ISBN 0-7414-1132-6
Library of Congress TXU-961-942

Published by:

INFINITY
PUBLISHING.COM

519 West Lancaster Avenue
Haverford, PA 19041-1413
Info@buybooksontheweb.com
www.buybooksontheweb.com
Toll-free (877) BUY BOOK
Local Phone (610) 520-2500
Fax (610) 519-0261

Printed in the United States of America

Printed on Recycled Paper

Published July, 2002

Message to the Reader

I debated with myself whether or not to release this book. I wasn't sure if sharing deeply personal material was wise. I thought it would do a lot of good because many people could relate to my experiences. I wondered if readers would take me seriously because of the young voice found in the poetry. I came to the conclusion that it was imperative to grasp readers and hopefully compel them to continue to read and grow with my material. In this book, you will see through the eyes of a young gay man beginning his journey through a hectic life filled with challenges and lessons.

I wrote these poems as a form of getting through tough times and venting my feelings. It wasn't until much later that I decided to release them all in the form of a book. Five Years of Solitary depicts the five years from the age of 17-22. I hope this book allows you to relate or take something valuable from it. I value all my experiences as a way of God guiding me through life. It's only the beginning so sit back, relax and enjoy. May God bless you as much as he has me.

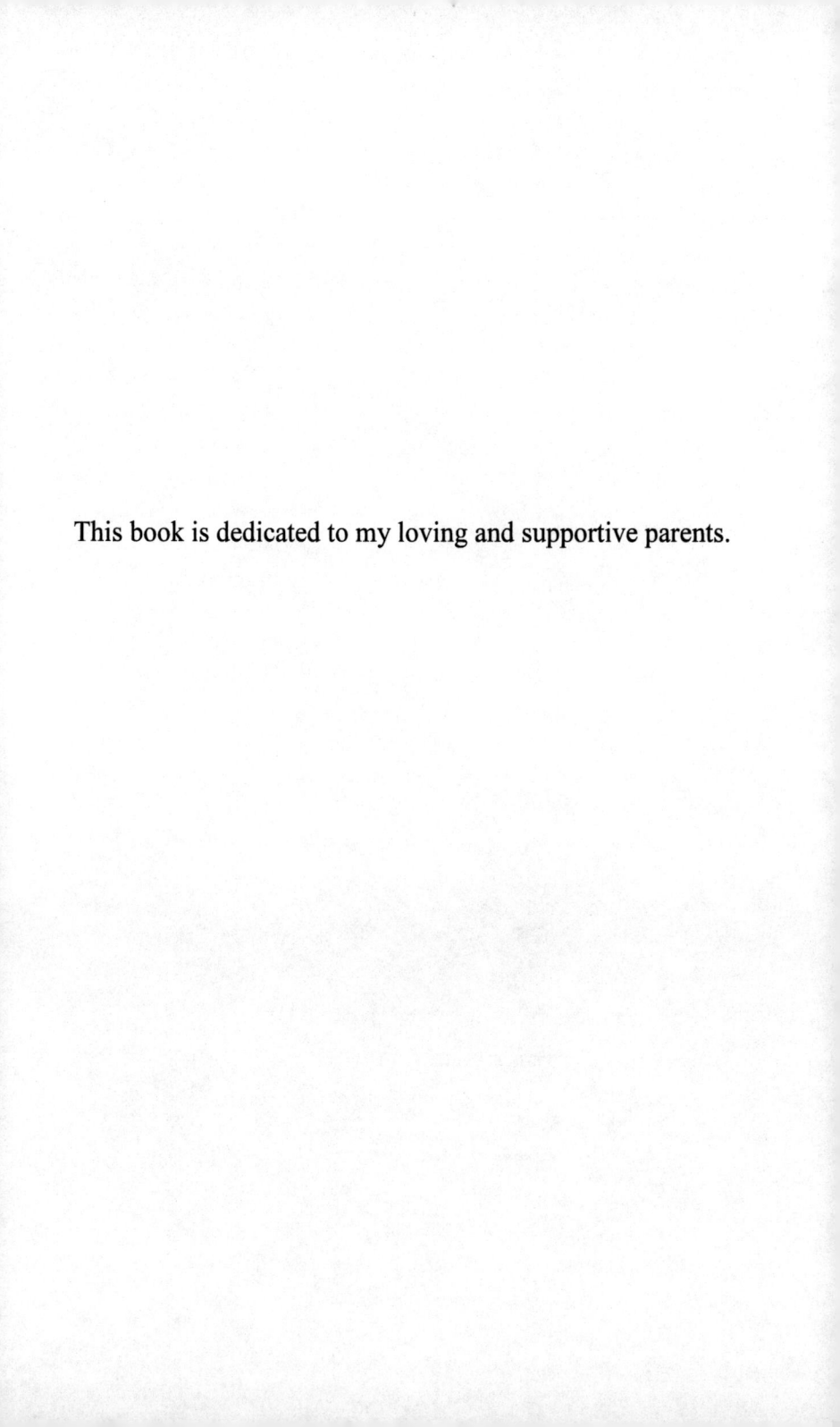

This book is dedicated to my loving and supportive parents.

Wisdom is the gift from the wounds I have endured.

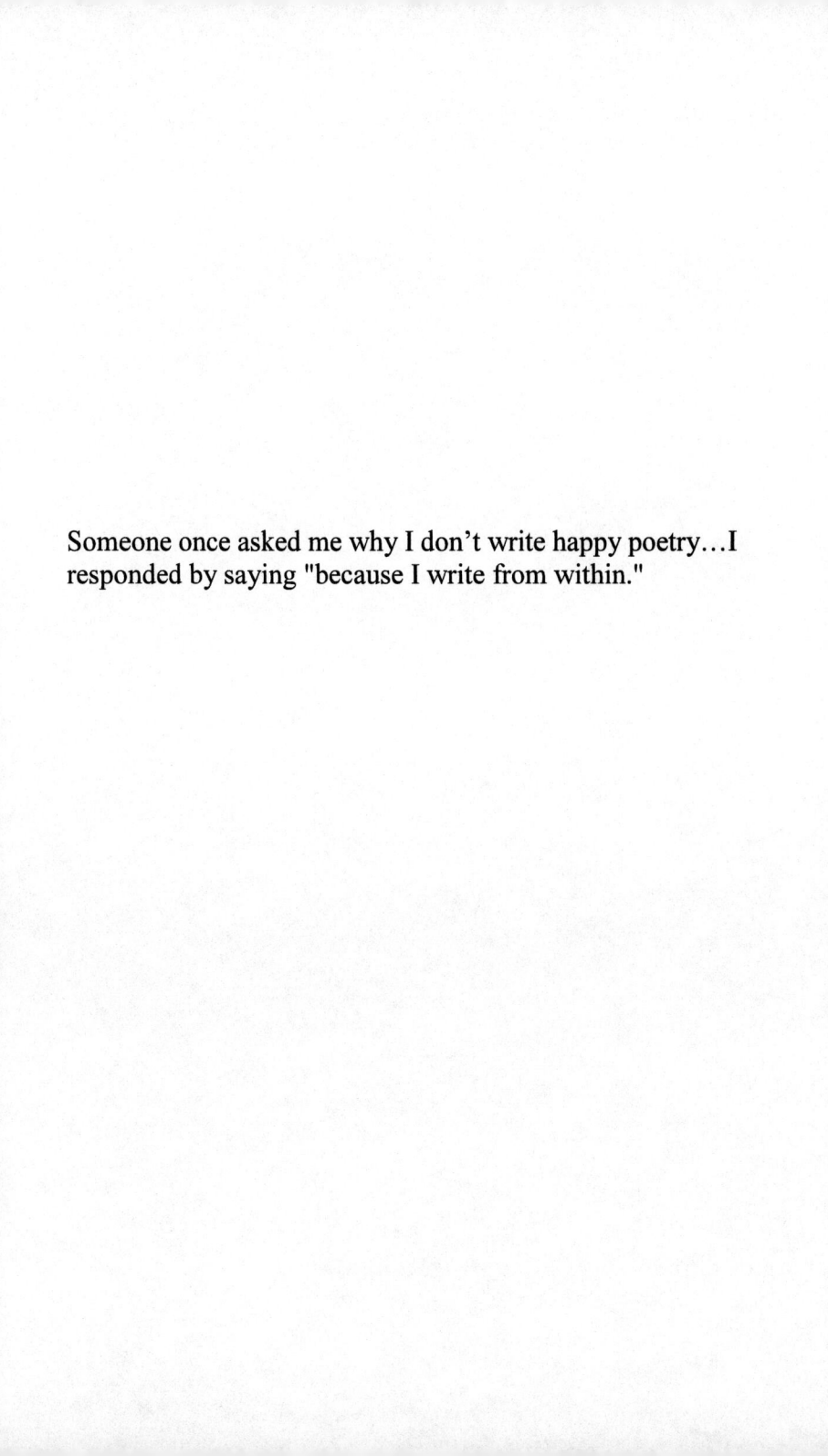

Someone once asked me why I don't write happy poetry…I responded by saying "because I write from within."

Foreword

Here it is: a continuation and rupture with the great traditions of Nuyorican poetry --- in your face and full of feelings. Five Years of Solitary has been a long time coming both in terms of hard earned experiences in the peculiar highways and byways of New York City's Gay Latino world and as a literary project. Elliot Torres is a new and sometimes quite disturbing poetic voice whose freshness and upfront tenor signals the beginning of a rich and productive artistic career.

During the last two years, I have been privileged to have an insider's view of Five Years of Solitary. Clearly, Elliot's work is part of an explosion of Gay Latino literary production that is giving voice to an experience that has in many ways remained untold. Fortunately, this self-published book is another path to bringing one of those voices to a wider audience of readers and writers. This collection has it all: love, personal pain, sex, hip-hop attitude, small town boy comes to Gotham, and the beginnings of a spiritual awakening.

Some of these poems will delight you, others will make you laugh, and others will make you angry. Welcome to Elliot's cellblock as well as his precisely executed escape plan. Those who are not afraid to feel, think, and love hard will find this small volume an uplifting adventure in words. I encourage you to travel the road that Five Years of Solitary is opening up and be assured that this is only the beginning. Paz y Luz.

Edgar Rivera Colon
New York City
March 2002

Table of Contents

The Scorpion 1
Waukegan, Illinois 2
Wanting 3
Superficiality 4
Screaming For Help in a Silent World 5
Being Alone 6
Haters In Disguise 8
When Will I? 10
The Darkness Within 11
Reflection 12
Where Does My Heart Reside? 13
Leaving the Anger Behind 14
Longing for A Smile 15
Where Am I to Go? 16
Destinations 17
Hollywood 18
My Depths in the Bahamas 19
My Time in Harlem 20
South Beach 21
San Francisco 22
South Bronx 23
A Desire 24
Your Heart 25
The Power of Rain 26
I Hope He Dies 27
Lights Out 28
Lost Soul 29
Whispers 30
Just Another Piece 31
Distant Friend 32
A Heart of Stone 34
The Calling 35
Mister Man 36
I'm Sorry 37
Alias: Sean 38
With Each Embrace 39
Reality 40

Rage	41
Us	42
Words	44
Home Wrecker	45
It Feels So Good	47
Endured	48
Control	49
******'s Bitch	50
Betrayal	51
That Very First Night	52
When The Tears Stopped Falling	54
Deep Pocket	55
Incarcerated	57
Goodbye	58
Why Then?	60
Rebirth	62
Alone	64
Unaware of the Game	65
Burst	67
Faded	68
No-Win Situation	70
What Could Never Be	71
Today I Saw the Light	72
My Cue	73
Unnecessary Pain	74
In The Bedroom	75
Homo Thugs	76
Numb	77
Passion & Desire	78
Issues	79
Memories of A Young Soul	80
Freedom	81
No Lasting Relationships	82
Voices & Opinions	83
Relations Gone Awry	84
Unconditional Love	85
175 Thompson	86
To Love Myself	87
Never Depart	89
Five Years of Solitary	90
Acknowledgements	93

The Scorpion

The scorpion leaves its burrow
To the harsh environment known as the world

It stings only when provoked
Wary of who comes near it or if it feels threatened

Its poison venomous
Dripping, awaiting predators who attempt to harm it

Determined and fearless of getting what it desires
The scorpion's thirst for happiness burns like fire

The scorpion, an incredible invertebrate
The scorpion is powerful and deep
Listen to what he has to say.

Waukegan, Illinois

What a place to grow up
Feeling trapped and suffocated
By the population of 77,000
I knew I didn't belong there
Where was I to go?
I couldn't breathe
I knew I had to leave.

Wanting

There is so much I want
I wanted it yesterday

There is so much I want
Don't come near me or stand in my way

I want it on a silver platter
Not a tray

There is so much I want
You decide whether you will go or stay

There is so much I want
In my mouth, in my pockets, deep inside
And I want it today

There is so much I want
I get down on my knees to pray
I stand still
Frozen
A mold of clay
I was so consumed with what I wanted
I almost wasn't around to enjoy another day.

Superficiality

I put my clothes on everyday
Only to realize that I will fall prey

Too many judgments from different walks of life
None knowing what I know and where I have been

To corporate America: They see a street kid with six tattoos who is up to no good but is good enough to offer sexual service to married men

To the beautiful young woman in the ghetto: She salivates at the mouth and sees me as her potential baby daddy. Studying me with the swiftness of a cheetah, she will stop at nothing to conquer me

To the homo thug: They see the next guy they want to sleep with for the night before they go selling themselves to older men or becoming an infamous fixture in Latin gay porn

But no one sees me and expects me to be a published poet, writer, successful, and to know what I want out of life

That's what I see.

Screaming For Help in a Silent World

I strive to reach the surface
So I can breathe

Everyone assumes I am happy and free
From loneliness and depression

They assume this because I have things pretty easy
And think I have nothing to cry about

I yell for help
But no one seems to hear the boy who they think has it all.

Being Alone

Being alone has become a way of life
Sometimes I feel my heart is being jabbed with a knife

I attempt to remain strong; I try all that I can
Will this strength last even though I don't have a man?

To love, hug, and care for me
To share good times but always let me be free

To be for real and steer free from games
My past is lengthy and tired of all the lames

I need a mature and successful man
Who knows what he wants and does what he can

To show me that he cares and is in it for the long haul
Who I can always think about and never dread to call

Who I don't throw out the morning after
With whom I can share a joke and much laughter

Who I can call my love with the passage of time
The one I will not dismiss like a measly dime.

I remember the first time my father said; "I love you".
How could I forget? I was twenty years old.

Haters In Disguise

Too often I run into a friend
You feel as though they will be there until the end

Yet you find that they have a dark shadow lurking in their soul
Eventually it will decay and take its toll

I am not to blame for the animosity you hold
It's there
I'm not blind
I've been told

I have many possessions you desire
I know it kills you
The envy
It burns like fire

Not once are you happy when I succeed
My failures nourishment for your ego
Keeps you satisfied indeed

From others I have experienced that hate
People too focused on material possessions
Yet no food on their plate

They want to wear labels
To make them feel content
It's deeper than that
They know nothing about happiness
And their money all spent

They believe things will change with the passage of time
When they will have more money and more possessions

Until then they have enough to hold them until later
But they choose to spend their energy on being a hater.

When Will I?

When will I?
Realize that love comes from within

When will I?
Know that I am not alone

When will I?
Experience unconditional love

When will I?
Wake up to a kiss from my partner

When will I?
Smile when I look in the mirror

When will I?
See the error of my ways

When will I?
Have the success that I crave

When will I?
Be happy

When will I?

The Darkness Within

The darkness around me seems like it does not want to end
I lay here thinking and crying
Wishing for a friend

I feel abandoned and alone
Not a sound around me
Not even from the phone

It's as though I have fallen off the earth and no one seems to know
I haven't eaten, haven't slept, only cried and my sorrow shows

I feel the pain that will not go away
The sharpness in my heart that just wants to stay

It is a reminder of the memories of the sadness in my life
Only to return like a criminal repeating a crime

There are plenty there that I tend to feel
It is telling me that this pain is for real

Who knows when I will overcome the pain and I will see no more darkness
The day when I can smile and feel all the happiness

Hopefully that day is near.

Reflection

I look in the mirror…
On the surface I like what I see

I have to be content with what lies within
So many times, so many sins, this is the story now let me begin

Can you forgive me God for the pain I have caused?
I evaluate everything and take a pause

The lashing out, rudeness, not a care in sight
I am selfish, self-centered, involved in many fights

So many confrontations I did see
What a waste of time
Several relationships I did free

I found myself alone in a dark room
One day it all hit me…Boom!

Life is too short to shit on people for satisfaction
Negative it is, not a positive action

It is now that I will see deeper than the skin
I will release the anger and start to grin

What matters is to be happy, not to be shallow with harmful intentions
Remember to be content, it's important when looking at your reflection.

Where Does My Heart Reside?

Where does my heart reside?
I sit and wonder and ask God why

Where does my heart reside?
I seek the answers, please tell me why

Where does my heart reside?
Beneath the surface, deep inside

Where does my heart reside?
So many questions
Needing answers
While no one is by my side

Where does my heart reside?
Confusion and loneliness
No one in whom I can confide

Where does my heart reside?
I live in my own world
Avoiding sunlight outside

Where does my heart reside?
Some day I will know
And I will smile.

Leaving the Anger Behind

I try to leave it behind
I remember I was innocent, sweet and kind

Why did they want to hurt me?
Joy they obtained but sadness I did see

I was beat and dragged through the ground
Today, trying to be nice is difficult I have found

Excuses I have to avoid
With my feelings and heart, they toyed

Rebuilding was a task in itself
I don't know if I can put the anger on the shelf

I am stronger than ever before
Too many times I was crying on the floor

Hitting the bottom was something I needed
Overcoming the fears is where I have succeeded

I will come out on top, this I know
I will be better and my soul will grow.

Longing for A Smile

The pain I felt was all too near
I always walked around thinking, always in fear

That the pain would return like morning
To wake me up from my sleep
I hope it doesn't return
I hope it doesn't creep

Behind when I don't expect it to come
To prick me like a needle to a thumb

I hope it doesn't return the pressure I felt in my chest
I feel it only happens to me and not to the rest

When can I feel the joy and happiness I long for?

Where Am I to Go?

I feel lost as I walk through the frantic metropolis

My surroundings swallowing me like a tiger grasps its prey

Suffocated by the loneliness

I seek refuge

The rain hitting me with a strong force reminding me I'm alive

No friends to cry on
No lover to hold on

I'm out on my own
Always wondering
Where am I to go?

Destinations

San Francisco, California

Looking in the distance I stand in doubt
Do I proceed or take another route

Unsure of what to do
I think to myself is this place false or true

I let go and follow my heart
Is it wrong, ignorant or smart?

I look ahead to the possibilities at hand
I sigh and think damn what a place to land

Making it to the end is the ultimate goal
I see it in my eyes and feel it in my soul

I'm almost there and look forward to something new
The peace, the scenery, but most importantly you.

Hollywood

Hollywood, California

The land of many famous dreams
Everyone has it in his or her eyes
Things are not what they seem

Going after their big break
Spare no expense
Everything is at stake
Even the personality which is often fake

Difference between fake and real
It's where your heart is
Not how you look on the following reel

Many hearts to steal
Too driven
To stop and feel

Hollywood…the land of make believe
And plagued with those who deceive.

My Depths in the Bahamas

Paradise Island, Bahamas

I look in the depths of the ocean and see a serene world beneath my feet. I see an array of life not caring about what is going on in our world. The fish swim through the water knowing they are being admired like a sleek fashion model. A stingray glides past knowing it is dominant and powerful. I see a dolphin paying as much attention to the boat as I am to it. It's displaying its humbleness showing that I am every bit as important as it is. The dolphin is not alone; there are other dolphins as well. It's as if it is trying to tell me something. I continue to view the depths beneath and absorb everything within.

My Time in Harlem

Harlem, New York

You are the dream I don't want to awake from
The one who shows me what a relationship is about

Treating me with kindness and respect
And bestowing an immense amount of affection on me

You listen to what I say with interest
My worries are yours and yours are mine

You care whether or not I am happy
And if I don't have a smile, the sight of you brings a grin

Your sense of humor brings me joy and laughter
Always a healthy feeling
I always want you near
Your warmth always present
Your heart always beating
Ah…us together
The way things should be.

South Beach

South Beach, Miami

Alone on the beach just off Ocean Drive
The sun feeding me life
Reminding me I'm alive

I needed to escape once again
Seeking answers that are all within

Unwilling to be open to any man who talks to me
Telling them to leave and let me be

Here I am
Ready to get back home
The answers aren't here
Hopefully soon I will know.

San Francisco

San Francisco, California

The city by the bay
Its beauty breathtaking
Damn…I don't know what to say

I almost fled to this majestic metropolis
Almost leaving NYC
Running away from everything
In search of something new

I looked for an escape from my life
I thought this city would be the answer

I formed close bonds with friends
Which will keep me linked to this city forever.

South Bronx

South Bronx, New York

Walking down the avenue
Not much runs through my mind except visions of you

I watch the haze of the morning rain
Awaiting the time
The end of the pain

The pain of the past where we let go as lovers
No longer a vision of future endeavors

When I look at you I see forever
You ask me
Will you leave?
I reply, never

You are a part of my soul
You walked away
And my heart you stole.

A Desire

Love was always something that eluded me. It was the one thing I always desired but couldn't seem to grasp. I have always been used to getting what I wanted but when it came to love I was not successful. It wasn't that I was not willing to give my heart out and put forth the effort necessary to make something work. The problem was that the guys I was meeting didn't feel the same way. They were looking for different things. I was looking for the guy who would give me his heart and enjoyed being around me. They were looking for the lay to hold them over to the next week. I know that point of view because I saw through the eyes that they do. I grew tired of that thinking and that lifestyle. I wanted to make a life with one man and love him. It just felt like I was the only one out there that felt this and there weren't any guys out there for me. They were all promiscuous and I just felt alone. I am not the type of person to give up but I did. I gave up hope of love because the gay life really discouraged me. It was telling me that there was no way I was going to meet Mr. Right. It was telling me that when I meet someone he will be sleeping with someone else when I'm not looking. It was telling me that I will grow old alone and I won't have the dream of one day living with my lover and building a home based on trust, loyalty, sharing, togetherness, humility, compassion, compromise, and overall…Love.

Your Heart

When in deep thought one day, I began to think about feeling the comfort of wool wrapped around me as each fiber briskly moved against my arms. The warmth brought a feeling of safety. Chills overwhelmed my body as I thought to myself that nothing could hurt me now. My ears could hear your heart beating and as I got closer the beats got stronger. I was in an atmosphere filled with happiness. That day I was in your arms. I hope that one day I can feel the same again. Only time will tell.

The Power of Rain

Greenwich Village, NYC

Walking home alone in the rain
Is nothing
Far from being insane

Being bombarded by the drops and cold
I look to my right and there is no one to hold

I brave these elements all on my own
Not expecting to hear the sound of the phone

I am soon approaching my destination
Will I continue to love?
Or hand in my resignation.

I Hope He Dies

I hope he dies
Those were the words that made me cry

I hope he dies
Tears of sorrow
Knowing that this guy I loved
Didn't want me to see tomorrow

I hope he dies
I stood with him even looked past the lies

I hope he dies
He was angered with me
I was the one he shoved and set free

I hope he dies
Those were the words I could not forget

I hope he dies
The words that let it be known
That when I threw him out
I stood strong, empowered, and alone

I hope he dies
He told a mutual friend
Words so profound
Love something I have found
Without him.

Lights Out

As I drown myself in bottles of Bacardi
I think to myself
I am getting tired of all of the parties

I lived the life for a short while
But that life lasted a short mile

It was filled with various clubs; it was such a scene
I got tired of it and put up a screen

Between myself and that fake world
I had to take charge of my real world

I used to take bumps of coke
Each one came with the social life that went up in smoke

As time went on I got tired and bored
I was ready to leave but made sure I scored

Sex was part of this very fast scene
I grew tired of the guys that I screwed and seen

I can't complain the sex was great
I don't think I'm ready for a mate
Often contemplating departing from this state

I took another route, which I couldn't lose
I walked away and blew out the fuse.

Lost Soul

Once, just once I was asked
How much time do you have?

Once, just once I responded
How much money do you have?

In the process, I lost my soul.

Whispers

As I walk by the trenches
I hear whispers

Admiration from players
Dissection from haters

Heads turn
And gossip churns

I am the subject of bickering
Enjoyable snickering

Why do they spend their energy dissing me?
Unhappiness has to be the answer
Eating them away like an incurable cancer

My suggestion
Live life and let me be
If you comply
Your hatred, anger and jealousy will be set free
But if you cannot
Take a deep breath and count to three
And remember
It's all about me
You've bestowed that power upon me.

Just Another Piece

So many young naïve faces in the scene
Hoping to be discovered
Only to fall prey to the sexual fiends

They give themselves up to the promoter, the door guy, and the DJ
All of which care less of what this young piece has to say

They feel as though they have juice because of who has come into their life
Sadly mistaken the piece is one of many on the list
Belonging to the trife

A lengthy game played by so many fools
Unwilling to stand their ground
And use their intellectual tools

Which become powerful in time
But too concerned on someone beating them to the climb

Of the social ladder
Where many necks are slit
The piece thinks he has made it to the top
Only to realize this life doesn't fit

In the end his soul was given one too many times
Listening to the noise of so many tired lines

An ego rises when a player buys him a new fleece
But in the end, he still remains just another piece.

Distant Friend

There you were to my surprise
Popped on my screen before my very eyes

So long ago, so much time has passed
This time we said our conversation would last

Where did it take us? A more serious route
So long it lasted, so much to talk about

Where to begin so much catching up
We continued as if long time friends who never gave up

You ask a question and I am pleased to answer
I add some humor to change the tone and transfer

To a different subject
So many we discussed
Only honesty and truth
In you, I can trust

Why is it I have only spoken to you and can be so open?
A mystery to myself but trust can be broken

By you I doubt
You seem as real as they come
So honest and opinionated
Where are you from?

Obviously somewhere you were taught
Right from wrong
Our conversation continues long and strong

Sarcasm, something you don't seem to lack
But tonight
You laid it to rest like a CD paused on a single track

We say goodnight and wish each other the best
Until next time
Our conversation is laid to rest.

A Heart of Stone

I once desired love
With the impatience of a young child wanting a toy

I displayed the kindness and gentleness
That was once a part of me

Over the years when relationships expired
I grew a numb feeling in my heart
Something not to be admired

Men would come into my life
Sometimes wanting one night
Sometimes wanting more
I explored both paths
Sometimes wondering what for

One path led me to broken hearts
The other breaking them right from the start

Each one gave me strength
To rise and gain wisdom

I was empowered
Despite being broken apart

At times lack of understanding left me alone
I had to let go of many things
And gained a heart of stone.

The Calling

I hear the bells at night as they chime
They are calling
All of the time

One night I am pursued and given great pleasure
A night when heated arousals take on a whole new meaning

The sweat drips down cooling our bodies
From the heat we continue to feel
That night the bells stopped calling
My sins were too much to handle so they called no more

They were calling me to do some good
But I was too good at being bad.

Mister Man

You flashed your career in my face
Thinking I would be impressed by who you were

High powered mister man
You wanted me on your terms
That was your plan

To sleep with you every two weeks
I was just another toy so to speak

I wanted more than I was getting
I was someone so easy to be forgetting

You thought I would be content with so little time
And so many dinners
I needed a real man

I was not impressed.

I'm Sorry

I'm sorry for caring so much
I was there for you whenever you needed me

I'm sorry for listening to your words
The ones that put me down to the earth

I'm sorry for waiting for your phone call
I waited for days but never heard your voice

I'm sorry for trusting you
Believing that you were faithful and I was the only one

I'm sorry for angering you
My apologies are in my bruises

I'm sorry for not understanding who you were
If I had known, I would have loved you less

I'm sorry…

I'm sorry I didn't leave you sooner.

Alias: Sean

I once knew someone named Sean
We bonded together
But not for long

He grasped his alias like someone drowning and gasping for that last breath of air

He was pleasant to be around and a joy to embrace
He presented masks to everyone
Giving them a fresh new face

I had no doubt that he cared
His friends annoyances
They couldn't be shared

I released from Sean quickly to his surprise
That's because I am real
And I bear no disguise.

With Each Embrace

I let go and release the wall
The barrier is gone
Crushed by the fall

I am wise
Educated by the pain
I have risen twice
Comforted by the rain

I will rise to give you my all
Fearless of the pain
Of another fall

You have shown me compassion and care with each embrace
I express my joy every time I see your face

We go together into the realm of the unknown
A bond made by God
Aware that we are not alone

The sound of your voice
Makes me feel safe and secure
I know what you speak is not tainted but pure

I have me a rare find
It's not everyday you run across someone of your kind

A sweet, romantic willing to show me a new place
I am yours and you are mine
I express it with each embrace.

Reality

I awoke one morning to find no one by my side
You had left and gotten off the ride

The dead of silence lay in the air
No longer will I feel the warmth of your stare

I am not used to being alone
Always accustomed to the ringing of the phone

I will have to cope with the absence of your heart
This was true right from the start

You were not fully with me another you did love
Someone you couldn't release, someone you couldn't shove

Today was the day that gave me great concern
I knew it was the day
You wouldn't return.

Rage

I have rage against you
I acquired it from my past

The many places
Several faces

It's killing me
Fast.

Us

I remember the day we first met
Looking across the street was something I couldn't forget

You were walking towards me with a glare in your eyes
Bright and vivid like the stars in the sky

I thought wow, could he be the one
Or is he around me just to have some fun

To my surprise, I experienced something like nothing before
I wish you could hug and kiss me and not ignore

As time progressed, so did the love we shared
It was so strong that nothing else compared

The first phase in this journey of love
Illustrated some obstacles that we were able to shove

At one point our future as lovers was no longer a reality
Now it's just a mere formality

Things are the way they are because it is meant to be
It made me joyous the day when you said…I see

The day you realized that we belonged together
Is a day we will always remember in our lives forever

The truth is that you mean the world to me and you are in my heart

You are part of my life and this is just the start

The beginning of our future together…the love…the passion…the trust…but most importantly forever
And when I look back to that night when we first met
There is only one word that sums it up…

        Us

Words

When I look into your eyes
Clear and sublime
I wish I could be with you all of the time

You are sweet and demure
I want no other
I am sure

There isn't a day that goes by
That I don't think about you
This is no lie

To be with you is a pleasure
No other guy could ever measure

To you, a man who I carry in my heart
I hope we never part

To see us together for a very long time
I hope you share this vision
Love isn't a crime

Assuring you that I am yours
I wouldn't have it any other way
So listen to what I am trying to say

I love you.

Home Wrecker

I am often approached by an attached male
Who can't be faithful and often fails

Who wants me kept on the side
As a forbidden secret he can hide

Who calls his boyfriend
After our two hours of sex
Reassuring his love, who informed
Would quickly become his ex

I am an accessory to this charade
He is paranoid of getting caught
Scared and afraid

The passion is too hot to resist
Love between them
Does not exist

My sexual needs met
My heart
I'd forget

I am hurting myself instead of loving
Rather than embracing him
I should be shoving
I never thought I would be loving

So strong and out of my hands
Like an ocean current drowning the sand

I walked away quietly when the time was right
With the serenity of a peaceful summer night

I wasn't surprised when he didn't run after me
No peaceful end could be expected
But when days and months passed and I heard from him
My lack of response left him rejected

I wasn't proud of coming between two lovers
I hold half the accountability
Chances of this happening again?
Zero probability.

It Feels So Good

It feels so good to finally let go
To know that tomorrow I wont be thinking of you
Worrying on whether or not you are faithful
And feeling as though I need you so much

It feels so good to have my peace of mind back
To love myself so much that I question why
I endured the pain for so long

It feels so good to be free
To be able to breath and wake up with a good nights rest
The sleepless nights and tension merely a distant memory

It feels so good to have myself back
To have the soul you took
Reclaimed! Back home where it belongs

It feels so good to love and be loved
To look in the mirror and smile
To be embraced and loved by someone who appreciates you

Love…

It feels so good.

Endured

Once I loved
Thought I would never love again

You were the reason…
I endured negative emotions

So many fights
So much lost time
Always alone
For so many nights

I reached the point
I could no longer pretend
I decided everything had to come to an end

I survived and escaped
Despite my soul was raped
You were the reason…
I endured negative emotions.

Control

I moved too fast you said
So I slowed down

I looked better with facial hair you said
So I grew a goatee

You liked me in certain sexual positions
So I obliged to make you happy

You said grip harder when I gave you head
So I grasped with my fist

I said stop but you kept thrusting your energy inside of me
So I wiped the blood from my ass

You said I was the one you wanted
So I said goodbye.

******'s Bitch

High powered exec
The meaningless relation
How easy to forget

Took me out to dinners to impress
With no stress
Especially when we had sex

Saw him every two weeks of the month
It wasn't enough
I wanted more
I was someone he wanted to explore

Gossip, something he enjoyed putting energy into
Discussing what we had done to a select few
Words get around
And so do you

I was young
Simply twenty
But I was informed and knew plenty

You were thirty-two
Thought you had one over on me
I was blinded but you made me see
You were fast
You knew when we met it wouldn't last.

Betrayal

So many times people enter our lives
Unexpected whenever another arrives

Friends, acquaintances, and lovers
Seeking refuge under the covers

Bestowing trust in many souls
Many mistakes which have taken their toll

I possess the knowledge of life, which has taken its time
Some things cannot be rushed
Like a distant mountain climb

The wounds I bear too many to count
Have healed over the years
I stand on the mount

I reflect on the past
My life, what a tale
Too many times I have been tested by betrayal.

That Very First Night

I saw you one day from afar
How good it was not to feel like a lie but instead a star

You treated me like a forbidden love
I have met the one who embraces me and we fit like a hand to a glove

You placed me aside like a book read many times and known all too well
Being with you wasn't pleasant, it wasn't heaven
It was hell

You are a great person but you have too much to learn
You will not hurt me anymore and I will not return

You had me in your arms tightly
But I reached and freed myself
I jumped!
I was off the shelf

The night that I met the guy who treated me like someone important
He treated me with care and respect
Not like a box of assortments

He treated me the way I always wanted to feel
I am in disbelief, is this for real?

Is this another one of my dreams?
Will I wake up and find it was all fake?
I hope not because my world he did shake

I thought wow, where has he been all this time
Living life, learning and preparing until this one night
When it all came together
When we knew it was real and it felt so right
Wow! How I could never forget
That very first night.

When The Tears Stopped Falling

I never thought the day would arrive
What I wanted to accomplish
For this I strived

They didn't seem to have an end or go away
I gave up, they've won, and they are here to stay

When oh when will they leave me for good
Lonely and depressed many times I stood

Please, I ask let me feel the joy
I am exhausted of this, of being a toy

Several I couldn't take seriously, players no doubt
The anger within me made me want to release and shout

Is it possible for the pain to stop calling?
It finally happened
And the tears stopped falling.

Deep Pocket

What I thought was the love of my life has departed
Because I refused to be a sugar daddy
I didn't realize love was about figures
If so, then, why even live?

I gave him my heart, my word, my time and my soul
I guess it wasn't enough because he took a stroll

Back to his ex the following day
He told me that was where he was going to stay

I accepted the fact of the loss of a mate
My heart wasn't enough; he wanted an hourly rate

Well, like I said I'm not a sugar daddy this is for sure
When I have love, I want it to be pure

He desires success, fame, fortune, and the world
He wants to buy
So do I but not because of some wealthy white guy

I look at the world, as I stand alone
Strong and secure like a solid fine stone

I will rise above the situation at hand

This is not to say I want to be shallow and mundane
Only respected and admired I hope they can sustain

Today is the day I cherish as I look to the days ahead
Relaxing with no worries lying on my bed

The sun gleams straight into my face
Reminding me that I am not alone if that were the case

I open the window and feel the warmth of the sun
I am ready for the journey; I am ready for the fun

To be alone is but to be strong
I know for sure that it won't be long

I received a call from the love that left me some time ago
He said he loved me

He went on to say that he left the other guy
And that I was the one; he wanted another try

I said, I love you for letting me go
I realized the love I yearned for was here

Its time for me to go, goodbye I said
I lay down with a smile and go right to bed

To wake up the next day with a smile
Something that took a while

But I have love, the love within
My name is Elliot, welcome, would you like to come in?

Incarcerated

Thoughts of you kept me in an emotional prison I found so difficult to escape from

No matter how hard I tried
I continued to be incarcerated

Until I freed myself from the shackles that caused me to weep on a daily basis, pass potential partners, and isolate myself from the outside world.

Goodbye

As he looked into my eyes
I could see that he loved me
Kind and caring
It could be no lie

As he looked into my eyes
I felt safe and secure
He was true to me
I was sure

As he looked into my eyes
I envisioned forever
And our love could not be severed

As he looked into my eyes
I think of the love that we shared
There were others but they didn't compare

As he looked into my eyes
I noticed he was staring at me no longer
But instead he was glaring at another

As I looked into my heart, I felt the pain and wounds
Time went by, I became stronger and he could hurt me no longer

One day he looked into my eyes
And was baffled
Hoping to be forgiven
He realized I couldn't be driven

As he looked into my eyes
His head fell down
Sad, disappointed, and overwhelmed
By my strength, power, and determination
Between us there could be no relation

As he looked into my eyes,
I smiled and said
Goodbye.

Why Then?

Why then?
Don't you see more in me

Why then?
Don't you see the vision I see; the future I desire

Why then?
Don't you see my soul through my eyes and realize that I am special

Why then?
Don't you see that I care for you
That you mean the world to me

Why then?
Don't we become one

I am special
I am special

Why then?
Do you pretend to rape me instead of make love to me

Why then?
Do you take me for granted

Why then?
Do you beat me with your words

Why then?
Do you ignore me like a forgotten memory

Why then?
Do you leave me alone helpless on the ground

Why then?

Rebirth

The tears that fall from the sky
Are the same ones from when I said goodbye

There is a difference
They are not tears of sorrow
They are of joy and looking toward tomorrow

The day when I realized I had the strength
Five months
Damn, what a length

Of time which I gave you plenty of
You were with the one who gave you money not love

You chose revenue over me
You are not the one, I can finally see

I have been here before
A repeated trip
Except this time
I didn't slip

I kept my balance, my strength, and determination
You and me
What a false combination

Times were difficult and good
Despite the pain
I still stood

By your side
While you drifted by the tide

The tide of wealth, security, and the good life
You saw it within your reach
You didn't want to move forward
Only maintain like a leech

You came into my life and taught me many things
For that I am thankful
I look forward to what the future may bring

I am free within
No longer shackled by the thorns that squeezed my heart
I see the light and relief
I am ready to start
The new beginning of my life
Rebirth
I am ready
It's time…

Alone

I thought you and I were forever
So many tears
When we were together

I loved you so much
I yearned for your every touch

So many experiences left me in the cold
My heart rock hard
I am cold
So I have been told

I went from sweet to unbearable
My past unforgettable
But also unregrettable

I am here today
Strong and alone
Not a sound from the phone
Not depressed
Not a moan

My future unknown
I believe happiness will be found within
And I will die alone.

Unaware of the Game

So accustomed to being the other one
So care free
I had my fun

I fell in love unexpectedly with him
I knew it wasn't right
I knew it was a sin

He was Puerto Rican just like me
His white boyfriend blinded or just didn't want to see

What was occurring over a year and a half
There was no sympathy on my behalf

I knew he would be mine despite he was taken
I would get my way
I wasn't mistaken

Eventually false promises and hopes took their toll
This is the baggage that comes with playing the role

Of the other man
Something I didn't plan

Until the day I knew it had to end
You loved me more than him
But I wasn't going to give you money
Only be your lover and friend

He gave you employment and took you on trips
Little did he know when he kissed you
He tasted my ass on your lips

One day, the whole charade crashed and burned
I walked away empowered
No longer naïve
I have learned

You and I knew what your man didn't
He believed there was nothing wrong
And everything was the same
That's because he was always
Unaware of the game.

Burst

You burst inside of me; quenching my thirst you grasp my face and kiss me. You taste the bitterness of my lips and smile because you just fed me and I fed your ego. You ask why I thirst for you and I tell you when you feed me from within we become one. You already are a part of my soul because the person you are and the time we shared. Our status together has come and gone but I will always remember the taste when you burst.

Faded

You say you feel a chill
The hairs on your arms are straight and still

You don't know where the breeze is coming from
It's the middle of the summer
But you grab your coke and rum

You still feel the cold
You and I are alone
It's making you stiff like a stone

You grab me closer to warm you up
Only to find that you drop your cup

You feel colder and colder
As your head lay on my shoulder

You don't know what to do
But you move away to see if it's true

As you move away you begin to feel warm
Comfortable heat
No signs of a storm

You find that I do not give you the warmth you desire
The love we shared finally grew tired

Of the situation that surrounded me
I finally closed up and I'm set free

I will never forget what we shared

You couldn't be there
Right then and there
Deep down
I know you cared.

No-Win Situation

You said you didn't like the way guys looked at me

You didn't like it when I wore a tank top so you asked me if
I would wear something else

When we walked down the street and guys said wassup to me
You got angry and attempted to grab my hand

When we hung out
You wanted me as your possession

When you hung out with your boyfriend
I rarely heard from you

How ironic.

What Could Never Be

You and I could never be
I kid myself over and over again but now I see

We are close friends, everlasting we say
At times I think we will drift apart some day

Your words that leave your body you claim as the truth
I believe they are lies detected by an expert sleuth

I love you so much but you have nothing to give
Lies, living in debt, infidelity, that's not how I want to live

We are the same age but worlds apart
I have seen so much and you are at the start

I envisioned forever
'Til death do us part
We could never be
But you will always remain
Deep within my heart.

Today I Saw the Light

Today I saw the light
It shined right in my face temporarily taking away my sight

Forcing me to examine within

What should stay? And what should go?
I know it's time to look forward
Forget the past, and continue to grow

I need to evolve to a higher level in this life

This I know.

My Cue

You said you were happy. I questioned why I stayed in this situation for almost two years. You and your boyfriend are moving forward and becoming a lot more serious. I have awakened to realize it's time for me to take my cue. Be strong, love myself, and know I can do better.

Unnecessary Pain

So much pain
How much more can I sustain

I am responsible for what I have become
So much darkness
When will I see the sun?

I have to learn to be with me
Blinded by the lies
Now I can see

No one can fill my void
I am exhausted and annoyed

My emotions a roller coaster gone awry
My patience strengthening
I take things day by day

22 years and no one has heard my cries
Or seen my tears
I never quit
Even after so many tries

One after another
I finally got it right
I am happy
I need no lover.

In The Bedroom

The room is spinning around me as I lay on the floor. The soothing music of Mary J Blige is playing in the background. My past flashes as reminders of what I did in the bedroom. The continuous raping of my soul and how many times it occurred. I gave myself away to so many men. One after another, each were very eager to get their chance at me. I look back and think, what did it all get me really? Well, I lay here in a dark room with a tear sliding down my cheek…in the bedroom.

Homo Thugs

So many I attract and date
Always players
Always late

Smoking blunts as a pastime
They reside at the bottom of the barrel
With no desire to climb

To rise above others low expectations
They take the easy way out
Unable to resist temptation
Charging for masturbation
Several cheap relations

They say they are all about me
Attempting to convince me
Unaware that I can see

Through the lies
Several sweet replies
Even more harsh good-byes

I always have to pull the plug
Often more
When I date a thug.

Numb

If you don't feel
Don't be intimate with me

If you can't feel
You can't touch

If you can't touch
You can't have

If you can't have
You can't desire

You can't desire
What does not exist.

Passion & Desire

I have known you for a very short time
And already you inspire a rhyme

How unexpected to meet as we did
What a pleasant surprise as I uncovered the lid

I opened up nervous and cautious to let you in
Enter a friend
Enter a grin

Sitting across at a table or lying on the bed
Wow! It feels so good just to hold your head

Near my heart which keeps beating
The passion in the air
I must be dreaming

I go with the flow and follow my heart
This was true right from the start

Waiting for the sign
When I would be yours and you would be mine

We've already spent some special times together
Laying on the bed
Wishing this time would last forever

You have an aura of realness, which can't be mistaken
I fall asleep in your arms
Hoping not to be awakened.

Issues

The finger is always pointed in my direction
You say I am the one with the issues but I am good enough
to take care of your erections

I don't need to hear your noise about how I need to change
Do some soul searching yourself and maybe your views will
rearrange

I told you I don't want to keep in touch
You stayed on the phone five seconds longer

I heard the dial tone
And moved on.

Memories of A Young Soul

I remember the days when the sight of a label
Made me feel good and stable

When walking into a club in the latest gear
Made me feel above all of my peers

When life was about the scene
I started early
Back when I was a teen

I was at a club Wednesday through Sunday
Not awakening until 7pm Monday

I got bored and walked away from it all
So I could regroup
Stand proud and tall

I sacrificed my social life for my education
Many nights alone
Having no relation

So much anger built within
So much pain
So much sin
But I hid it all beneath a fake grin.

Freedom

I mistook sex for love
I asked for guidance from above

I couldn't give myself over anymore to another
I hurt myself more
I suffered

I had to release the demons
To make room for the gifts
God has in store for my life

I feel the freedom of having the shackles removed
From my body
The weight of five years is lifted

The need for a man to fulfill my void…gone
The yearning for attention…gone
The pain of being lonely…gone
The days spent contemplating suicide…gone
The days spent crying in a dark room alone…gone
The self love necessary to live and be content…born.

No Lasting Relationships

I have gone through many men
Yet not one lasted more than three months

Not one said, they saw a lifetime with me
Not one said, they saw the next six months with me
Not one said, they saw the next month with me
Not one said, they saw the next week

All asked, where are the condoms?
All said, suck my dick
All said, they desired me
All said, I was the best sexually

Not one said I love you always and meant it.

Voices & Opinions

Too many voices
Too many opinions telling me what I should do

The answers are within despite what they say
Family and friends trying to assist and lead me a different way

I have to follow my heart and walk at my own pace
At times I make a wrong turn and arrive at a challenging place

I depart each with wisdom and strength
Each distinct in challenge and length

My experience all unique
What can I say
Too many voices and opinions
Relax!
God will guide me on my way.

Relations Gone Awry

I have been told that I have an angel's heart
And the devil's blood
They come together
Like grass and mud

I am me
And have become a product of my experiences
I attempt to be kind and smile
I am bitter and reside in denial

I can't seem to hold on to a relationship
So many come and go
It's taken me time
To learn to let go

I have been accused of having a bad attitude
Sometimes nice, sometimes rude
Often embroiled in several feuds

Attention of which I need plenty
Not as much now
As when I was twenty

I have many expectations
Which explains why so many didn't try
And my relationships have gone awry.

Unconditional Love

You were the one I loved
Despite the pain and disagreements
You were the one I loved

The good times we shared
Joy and happiness in the air
You were the one I loved

You were sweet and so caring at times
You were the one I loved

Other times you didn't want to be around me
You were the one I loved

I gave myself fully
You were the one I loved

You turned your back to me
I was still there
You were the one I loved

You said it was over
Who am I to love?

I found love like no other before
It replaced you and gave me more

It was from within
I found myself and unconditional love.

175 Thompson

I am free from the cell
It began as a heaven but became a hell

Many days spent alone not a sunlight to cherish
Four years
How I seemed to perish

Until the day I found the escape
In a place unexpected to myself

I arrived and have regained my soul
But the four years took their toll

So many turns of the knob
So many guys to forget
So much experience
Not one regret

My story lengthy and began in one place
175
And I left without a trace.

To Love Myself

The release of the tension within
Letting go of the pain, letting go of the sin

Where does the pain reside?
So easy to blame others
So easy to hide

It's been in me a very long time
I'm ready to let go
I'm ready to climb

The mountain of dreams and desires
I know I can get there
I know I can go higher

I have the strength of a thousand men
It's in me
I express it with my pen

In this world, so much bitterness and hate
I'm getting rid of mine
I hope it's not too late

I have been pounded to the ground more than once
By so many masks
So many fronts

I need to discover realness and truth in others
To have them by my side like sisters and brothers

My journey has taken me to places too familiar to me and unknown to others
I've evolved with each lover
Where the pain hovered

One day it all came to a conclusion
It was when I made the resolution
To love myself.

Never Depart

I am no longer bitter about my past
I have conquered it
I knew it wouldn't last

I went from a young soul seeking a mate
To a wiser young man looking no more and leaving it to fate

I realized I couldn't be consumed on whether or not my relationships would survive
Too many ended with distant good-byes

I have seen a lifetime through my twenty-two year old eyes
So many people amazed I have been with so many guys

One after another believing he could be the one
My smiles masks of the truth
I wasn't having fun

This life is a struggle
Yet a game to some
Unwilling to evolve from a player and falling victim to what others become

The truth is we all desire love
Sometimes it comes through people who embrace but prefer to shove

Beneath this life lays several broken hearts
Please realize love comes from within
And from yourself you will never depart.

Five Years of Solitary

The darkness how I know it so well
It took me a while to stand after I fell

Countless, what an expected number
To go through and still no lover

Everywhere I looked
Another wanted me hooked on his zipper
So he can have me and tear my heart
Like Jack The Ripper

Eighteen/Nineteen
Waking up and rinsing my mouth with Listerine

Innocence long gone back when I was eleven
Desire for happiness as if though in heaven

I searched for it in so many eyes
They didn't see the same
As my tears fell from the sky

Twenty/twenty-one
I feel old inside
I've lost; they have won

So alone
No one to hear my cries

Betrayals, mistrust, and lies
From friends and so many guys

I gave up on the search and yearned for sex
It didn't last long
I was too complex

I had to admit to weakness and seek salvation
But not in another sexual relation

I began to see the light
Not only during the day
But also at night

I began to stand alone, secure and content
So many people I have hurt for this I repent

In my dreams, God tells me it's time
So I gear up and prepare to climb

22 I see it near
Approaching soon
I have no fear

Higher education of which I have no more desire
It's almost over
The burning of the fire

Many accomplishments I have completed
Many more ahead
Something that will be repeated

The future brings many events
My past has prepared me for whatever presents

Itself in my life
Which has been so scary
I will never forget
My five years of solitary.

Acknowledgements

I would like to take this opportunity to thank God, St. Jude, my loving and supportive family, relatives and close friends. Thank you all so very much for being there. You all know who you are.

Special Thanks: To my lover, best friend, and heart A.T. You have shown me that true love is a reality and I am so thankful and feel blessed that God has brought you into my life.

Cover Photo taken by Olga Maria Benitez

Back Cover photo taken by: Daniel Sedano

Five Years of Solitary was edited by Edgar Rivera Colon

Be sure to visit www.ElliotTorres.com to learn more about the author, the latest on his current and future projects as well as an extensive photo gallery.

Thank You